Published 2025 by Mark Time Books UK
ISBN 978-0-9935033-4-4

Printed by barringtonprint
www.barringtonprint.com

Thirza Clout grew up in Kent and Wales and now lives on the English/Welsh border in Shropshire. For five years she was Chair of the Board of Wenlock Poetry Festival after careers in journalism, as a stand-up comedian and as a director for a conservation charity. In 2016 her first chap book, The Bone Seeker, was published by Mark Time Books UK and she won the Poetry Prize at the Doolin Literary Festival in County Clare. In May 2019 her second pamphlet, Aunts come armed with Welsh cakes, was published by Smith Doorstop, chosen by Carol Ann Duffy in her Laureate's Choice series. Percy and Grace is her first full collection.

Mark Time publishing was set up by award-winning Australian poet Ross Donlon to encourage emerging poets and foster the development of established poets. It is an invitation-only press and since winning the Wenlock Festival International Poetry prize in Shropshire Ross has extended his network of poets from Australia across the UK. From his home in Castlemaine, Victoria, he organises regular online and in person readings.

MARK TIME BOOKS UK

Come celebrate with me Percy and Grace
who raised three children and tried their best.
What more should we ask of our parents?

Contents

A Terrible Resolution

This is the year I must declutter - not in a kiss-arse
every sock gives me joy kind of way,
not in a tidy house tidy mind smug-arse kind of way,
not in a bloodless tight-arse minimalist kind of way;
I shall declutter in a totally bad-arse kind of way.

This will be the year I rip the guts out of ancient carcasses
kept mouldering too long in the dark under my bed.
This is the year I smash every cup and saucer Granny left
just as cracked and crazed as she was at her end,
burn unread all the letters from my father my mother kept
blaze them on a bonfire – make them vanish into ash.

Portrait of the writer's parents
after Gainsborough's Mr and Mrs Andrews

Mr and Mrs Percy and Grace
compose themselves against the backdrop
of their black-tarred henhouse
fringed by nettles

Mr and Mrs Percy and Grace
are wearing their best clothes
(her warm coat chosen to last -
his wedding suit still a little too big)

Mr and Mrs Percy and Grace
did not keep a horse
but the artist paints in a donkey
breath steaming from his innocent nose

Mr and Mrs Percy and Grace
never had a dog but the artist sketches in
a labrador straining towards
some treat it will never be allowed to eat

Mr and Mrs Percy and Grace
had a black cat – there with her leg up
and licking her backside
half-closed yellow eyes giving a look

Mr and Mrs Percy and Grace
had two older children - the artist
keeps the siblings for another painting
imagines dark angels hovering over a crib

not Gainsborough for that she thinks
maybe an Adoration after Giotto
in a mash-up with Hieronymus Bosch
with just a touch of the Brothers Grimm

prologue from their future

EXPLOSIONS
above a Canterbury bomb shelter
threw Percy and Grace together
they clung on
through years of after-shock

well
that was Grace's story
though Percy's sisters sniffed out
the whiff of fibs

Percy was born lucky -
with a hare lip and cleft palate
in a family where several babies died
he was lucky to survive

lucky to believe
this world would one day soon
require from each according to their means
give to each according to their needs

Grace was lucky too
luckier than her younger sisters
Joan and Mary
two dead babies she never mentioned

at fourteen Percy plunged his lungs
into the dark beneath South Wales
Grace boiled fruit in a Kent factory where
wireworms put her off jam for life

he was thirty three and she
was on the shelf at twenty-eight
food was rationed
they saw cities bombed

London blitzed and closer to them
Canterbury, Chatham and Newbury too
they did not know what would happen
if Hitler won

Percy and Grace
each wanted to find a mate
to bring children into this world
before it was too late

so
when no-one could swipe right
how did
Percy and Grace really meet

Grace asks

why must his sisters pry
he's not a little boy

he's thirty three years old
he doesn't want

to die childless
and a virgin

I don't want to die
childless

together we can make a home
have a family of our own

In the beginning

Despite the Blitz or perhaps because of it
as death keeps falling so close
the Marriage Bureau business soldiers on.

26 Charing Cross Road,
close to Leicester Square Tube Station.

Dear Miss Clout,

If you decide to join it will be necessary to state:

1.   Your permanent address i.e. Parents or near relative.
2.   The position your Father holds or held.

The fee is three guineas upon registration
£10 when you are suited to one of our clients.
The gentleman invariably pays
the latter amount for the lady.

We offer discreet advertisements
typeset in lead for Matrimonial Post
and Fashionable Marriage Advertiser.

Yours faithfully,

R. Charlesworth Ltd
Established 1860.

Grace writes her profile

height: five foot three
love of: music, children, cooking
religion: R.C.
income: yes
capital: small

She added inches to her height
lied about her love of children
definitely lied about the cooking

Did anyone else pay
to meet Miss Clout?

In the year before she received Percy's details
did she wonder if she had wasted three guineas
while she was nursing all hours and still to pay
not just bed and board but for uniform too?

Kent was full to bursting in 1941
so many young airmen desperate to fuck
careless if they sowed seed
before they flew into the void.

Years later Grace would hint at loves and losses
sometimes implying a man not free
other times a tragedy she could not speak of
always narrating herself as a Woman of Mystery.

Littlebourne Woods

1961

there they were great pools of bluebells
reflecting a perfect May sky
just as she had glimpsed them yesterday
as the school bus carried her home

she loves the thought of her mother's surprise
pictures her smiling as she lifts down
her favourite glass jug from the mantlepiece
so happy until she heard Grace scream

1940

he pulled over at Littlebourne   I wasn't suspicious   it was an air raid

he said he was taking shelter   I thought he was keeping us safe

I should have fought more   I kept saying no   I was crying   he wouldn't stop

afterwards he wound down the window   the smells made me feel sick

        he tried to kiss me   I pushed away his slimy mouth   he ignored me

going back took hours   he wanted to see fires   see where the bombs landed

        he said Goodnight Grace   as though nothing had happened

every day I worked my shifts counting
waiting for my blood to appear
stole quinine from the dispensary
bought more from two chemists in Canterbury
on my day off I swallowed the lot
endured pain and cramps before I passed
what may have been a clot though I believe not

Dear Miss Clout

I appreciate the frankness
with which you write
with regard to your religion.

I am in no way prejudiced
although I believe that
Roman Catholics accede
no validity to any denomination
other than their own.

Regarding the other
I quite realise you would not wish
to marry anyone without
having developed some feelings
in the matter.

I should be glad to receive
a photograph and will forward
one of my own - I am not what
might be called 'good-looking' but 'plain'.

I would be delighted to hear from you
if you are still interested.

dear dad

in my opinion you're lucky
Miss Clout saw no red flag

now I know why
Sundays were so grim

you scrubbing floors while Grace
incinerated a leg of lamb

I was shocked years later when she shouted
that you - my always upright father -

had broken your pre-nup promises
that you - my always pacifist father -

once threw a priest out of the house
were stone adamant that Catholics

would hold fast any child they caught
before the age of eight

said your children must be free
to choose when they grew up

now as I fumble for coins or notes
to give away in streets

Jesuit Dad you hold me fast
your priest was Marx

jigsaws

there's always too much sky
too many stones and walls
hard to pick out shapes
to complete the picture

Grace told me once that Percy
was born with a hare lip and cleft palate
his mother and all his sisters
never mentioned it nor

confirmed that it was Grace
who persuaded him to grow across the scar
that little ginger moustache
that salted all Dad's bristly kisses

Kent: Percy courts Grace

Nowhere in England I believe offers so much and so varied country
far-stretching orderly orchards, long-furrowed ploughed fields
rich pastures, the woods and the sea.

There are few lanes and roads I have not walked or cycled
on solitary rides. I have played football and cricket too
in most of the towns and villages. Especially I love

to ride down to the marsh district - Westmarsh,
Goldmarsh and Walmestone at dawn of a summer's day
all have a special glory.

I was last near Sandwich with my mother in June
when Canterbury was bombed.

bombing raid June 1942

the whole world seemed in eruption
away over Canterbury the sky
was lit up with a huge red glow
the heart of the glow was
a lighter red
more concentrated
clouds of smoke rose and lifted
white at first as they were reflected
in the bomb flashes
before they turned red, deep red
then lurid reddish black
rising to become
a sinister overpalling inferno
thunderous roars
screams of planes
slashed the air
combining to form a cacophony
as a base to it all
the thump
of ack-ack guns

this went on as I stood there
for an aeon
then I became conscious
of the cessation of noise
it died as quickly as it had risen
only one lone plane was circling
acting as the all-clear

on the horizon
I could still see the inferno
of Canterbury

here a few short miles away
the moon laid a splendid lustre
on fields where the dew
was forming
a sound broke the stillness
a few yards from where I stood
a nightingale began singing
such thrilling notes

Orchestration

You say you often wished to learn to play the violin Grace. For some years now I have done very little playing. Landladies are not always as tolerant as one could wish. I did not start to learn until I was 21 but eventually thanks to my teacher, a grand old man and still a friend, I managed to grind out a tune in the Orpheus orchestra in Dover. I must confess sometimes I did little more than make a sham though next to an old gentleman who was an expert on oboe and bassoon I played with abandon, knowing he would cover up. Other times needed careful attention. You can't think what a fool one feels to miss a pause sign and go on playing when the rest of the band has stopped.

hares

living in the village of Inkpen
gives me four miles
to cycle to work each evening

I can observe creatures
as they set out
on their night's forage

twice last week a young hare
went scampering in front of me

I slackened to give him a chance
to scramble up the bank
each time he too eased up
disappearing at last
through a gateway

the third night he brought a mate
the two of them repeated
the performance and both
appeared to enjoy it immensely

this week there have been three
as soon as I increased speed
they did likewise
when I got off and stood still
they stood still too
I could swear they were disappointed

last night for the first time I saw no hares
two great white owls were flying

swifts

at my lodgings there are a number
of swallows' nests and swifts

the latter are the most amazing
in that they never touch earth

even at night they simply rest
clinging to walls using their tails as props

feeding their young they fly continually
their energy must be tremendous

                              reading your letter dear father
                              I see your tremendous energy

                                    always on the wing
                                    capturing food to drop

                              into the beaks of your chicks
                                            open or not

                              at the end air could not lift you
                              black cylinders tethered you to earth

Percy arranges the first date

I will be wearing a grey suit
grey trilby
light brown waistcoat.
Could you let me have some
details of your probable attire
such as coat colour?
I am looking forward to meeting
albeit leavened with fears
of my not being suitable.

I am not a great
conversationalist
on first acquaintance
and must beg you beforehand
for a little indulgence
for my shyness.

The gap

Unique in his chain of letters
a four-day gap follows.
Is it possible
that the two of you
found a place to stay?
Found privacy to enjoy
that time
when new lovers assume
no-one else knows
the pleasure they find?

Could that be
what Percy means in his
next letter?
He tells Grace that she
made so easy what I
feared would be so difficult.

I cannot know what
either of you thought,
only try to understand
what you each found.

First date imagined

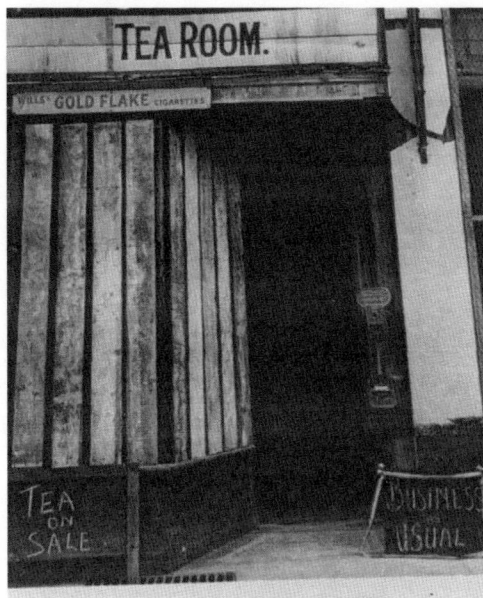

After you met outside the fever hospital
shyly recognised descriptions of clothes
hurried away to escape prying eyes,
where did the two of you go?

Percy feared your meeting would be
awkward. Would it be worse now?
You exchanged a single photo
could not curate multiple images. Maybe

in October 1942 you found it easy
to agree to go to a teashop
whichever teashop was still open
in the ruins of Canterbury – perhaps

you chose the one The Kent Messenger
featured four months before when
chalk boards declared it had TEA ON SALE
definitely BUSINESS AS USUAL.

The photograph lies beneath a story
about a blind woman who had made
a system for winning at village whist drives
still happening in Kent as bombs fell.

The day after the raid which left
79 people dead and the cathedral
only saved by four firewatchers
(all volunteers too old to fight)

that day the editor chose to make
front page news of a blind woman
keeping score at whist - alongside
Hitler's revenge for Cologne.

A proposal of marriage can be

a trail of gas scrawled across the sky
a whisper on a romantic evening
deeply eye to eye over a taverna table
or while holding hands under
red-checked cloths of trattorie in Roma
Bologna or Rimini or while eating
so much more expensively
undersea in the Maldives. Holidays

now top the league for the most
frequent moments to propose followed
by the icing on the cake at birthdays,
writing in sand upon a perfect beach,
on an anniversary – at Christmas,
on Valentine's Day in a heartbeat
or during any special meal despite
the risk of swallowing the hidden ring.

Some lovers propose on radio or TV
some gather friends and family
swear them to secrecy before
they take hostage the one that they desire
proposing so publicly
their victim is unable to refuse,
too shocked to say on camera
the tears they shed are not from joy.

Percy could not afford to wait,
could not create an occasion,
could not even be with Grace to go
down on one knee. He knows they both
have paid their fee to Charlesworth's
knows that Grace wants to marry
and so does he – six days after they meet
he declares he feels emboldened to propose.

They are of an age to know their minds
have similar interests and tastes,
his capital is thirty pounds, his income
three pounds and ten shillings a week. If
they marry before April the fifth
there will be an income tax reduction.
At the end of his proposal he adds
he will do all he can to make her happy.

Inkpen
N. Newbury
Berks. 27/1/42

Dear Grace;

Many thanks for your very welcome letter. I cannot fully say how delighted I am. Since last Saturday I have thought over everything & feel sure you & I could be very happy together. We have many mutual tastes & have enough commonsense & are both of an age to know our own minds. Now, since recieving your letter, I am emboldened to ask, will you marry me, Grace?

Perhaps this is rather blunt

Percy's proposal after their first meeting.

Wedding day, January 9 1943

The dress Grace wears is the something borrowed
for good luck. A horseshoe and a satin heart
weighted down by wishes for happiness, hang
beneath the white chrysanthemums she carries.

A pale buttonhole barely lightens the darkness
of her mother Maud – but Henry looks happy
as if glad to give away his only living child.

Beneath a coronet of satin flowers Grace squints,
without thick-lensed glasses her eyes, mole-blind,
look naked in the camera flash. On her special day
the bride must be seen although she cannot see.

Beside her sits the Matron of Honour, friend
and first wearer of that dress, maybe wondering
should Grace be wearing white, even second-hand.

Percy, who described himself 'plain featured
and not what you would call good-looking',
has scrubbed up well in a suit, the trousers
only slightly baggy, face almost handsome.

Jim serves as best man although he has not met
his brother's bride before. Their widowed mother
sports a stylish hat, a light coat of sprightly checks.

Portentous folds of velvet frame them in a studio
still looking straight to camera after eighty years.
I am looking back, developing my ideas of them
fixing them in black and white and shades of grey.

Bath

Jane Austen scents the honeyed air of crescents
where lovers stay, relaxed and renewed
by spa waters the Romans famously enjoyed.

Weekenders walk off three-star tasting menus
stroll through crowds fashionable enough
to please the elegant shade of Beau

which promenades around the Pump Room
passes through streams of European teens
bored by the subjunctive and busy sexting.

This city is a romantic choice for lovers now
to lie entwined in high-thread cotton sheets.
Not so for newlyweds who had to stay
with his sister as they can't afford to pay.

Breech: 1950

Twice she caught buses twenty miles to hospital
two hours each way with three changes
waiting on swollen feet at stops without seats
standing heavily in the heat of that July,
endured gloved invasions to swim me round.
She often told anyone how quickly I flipped back
kicking her womb as she carried her burdens home.
Especially she loved to emphasise how her waters broke
while she was serving groceries in the village shop.
Contrary from the start, that was her punchline.
I turned myself around to leave - head first I pushed
away from her. With her thumbprint she signed my navel
tenderly she pleated my newborn skin
taped on an old penny to mend the umbilical hernia.

Mother's arts

Mother was an alchemist. She conjured
magic from Dettol ointment and Lucozade.
At the first sniff bruises faded, grazes healed.

With silver instruments she cut holy strips
from a reel to seal squares of gauze. When
measles or a bilious attack struck one of us

she was at her best, no good hidings given
nor tears before bedtime threatened. Instead
Grace ascended bearing the bottle to the bedside

of the fortunate child, crackled back cellophane,
poured out gold. With great cunning I hid from her
my worst wound, scrawled mute hieroglyphs
in silence nursed a burning stone.

breathing difficulties

smog in our living room made it hard to breathe
smoke drifted from Grandad Henry's cheroots
wet and soggy at the mouth end

I was not allowed to say out loud
I was disgusted when Grandad draped
his snot-soaked hankies to dry on the mesh fireguard

I threw myself in tantrums to the floor
was punished when I said out loud it was unfair
he cheated at dominoes to beat me

an obese toad he squatted in our front room
it smelled of his commode
although we never said so out loud

he took any chance to escape his daughter's care
step by step on his metal crutches
waddled half a mile uphill to the Palm Tree pub

Grace and Percy weathered his accusations
nobody believed Percy had stolen
Grandad's store of Victory Vs

sixty years after his death
I keep one linen handkerchief
embroidered with an elaborate H

remember how every Christmas
he sang songs from the music halls
and laughed with Grace at how her mother Maud
disapproved when he took her to the Chatham Empire

Maud: 1954

eyes blind
your fingers
make needles fly

I don't know
what you knitted
sitting little and kind

in the armchair by the fire
with your bag of wools
and furry toffees for me

wearing maroon
or enveloped in
some darker cloth

when you disappeared
leaving grandad
in our front room

how long was it
before you died Granny
and what killed you

your own addled brain
or cruelty in your last home
the County Lunatic Asylum

*'abuse...neglect...degradation
... too much ECT was used
on some patients'*

Granny Clout
these official words too late
strike blows to the heart

saying

at teatimes the two of you
said it so often I thought
it was just a saying

when two women
pour tea from the same pot
one of them will have ginger twins

until I read your letters Percy
found that the two of you
before you even wed

joked of making ginger twins
so when you talked of them
above the heads of us three kids

(the ones you did make together
with not a ginger one among us
though we had ginger cousins aplenty)

Percy you must have been
winking at Grace
and she winking back at you

I never wanted ginger twins
when fertility fails me
I wield the teapot and smile

as if to welcome them
laugh as if at emojis they send me
from a parallel universe

tell them to keep out of the sun
tell them how very much
I would love them

Treat

When Dad thickly buttered
a slice of white bread, spooned

on sugar, tipped it to and fro
over the china bowl

he showered down so much love
it snowed across the cloth.

I licked my first finger, pressed down
to stick grains, licked again.

In our house love came granulated
never enough to be wasted.

time warp: 1942 and 1988

two miles from Inkpen one hill stands out
crowned by a stone needle

the hill of the White Horse
now blacked out by turf of course

        the National Trust carer for this land
        strides easily ahead of me
        up the slope of Cherhill Down

        up and on towards
        the White Horse
        newly re-chalked once again

towards Oxford you see
a well-wooded vista
Smallbourne and Ham sprawling west
the road climbing out
and on towards Salisbury

        he is excited to explain
        the wart-biter cricket
        was feared extinct
        but is newly rediscovered

        his sheepdog Bran sits
        lolls his tongue
        as I heave breath into my lungs

this land has no comparison
with the beauties of Kent
yet gives me a feeling
of quiet satisfaction

        Percy I wish I had known
        you trod here too

        it is you I want to tell
        about the renaissance
        of the wart-biter cricket

hair 1

Grace told me often
that as a child
her hair was blonde
darkened as she aged

she remained proud
her hair was mostly brown
when she died at seventy-nine

now Helen weaves
streaks of blonde
into my hair

lightening the brown
covering the grey
I am not ready for

I tell Helen
I have my mother's genes

hair 2

it is your colour Percy that I crave
remembering you were patient

as I plaited your hair
tied it with scarlet ribbons

you stayed still as if sitting for Titian
a painter I had not heard of then

he could have captured
the shades and colour of you

hair 3

that winter when pneumonia
combined with pleurisy
kept you shivering beneath blankets
diminishing within your bed
November right through to February
your hair turned white as you fought for breath

months later when we knew you'd live
we feared your scalp was dirty
before we saw it was colour returning
first brown then red at the roots like you

owl and robin

Percy writes of great white owls he sees
as he cycles to night shifts in Hungerford

his sweetheart Grace describes
robins hopping outside her window

desires to mate and nest
flutter through their letters

                              aggressive and territorial
                              my mother Grace is always

                         one of the last to stop singing at night
                         one of the first to start the dawn chorus

            their granddaughter is a mother herself
            believes robins hop into her life

            when she needs comfort
            from the Nana Grace she mourns

                              in my garden robins scrap and sing
                              barn owls hunt through the dusk

viewing

death-masked in pink foundation and blusher
Percy's face shocked me

Grace flung herself onto the coffin
drifts of white nylon enfolded the doll of him

I breathed in formaldehyde and heard
sobs heaved from the deepest seam of Grace

had no idea what I could do
to comfort her

did not know how to grieve
my dear and absent dad

A present

The last gift my mother gave to me
was her death

she did not linger at the threshold
nor wait six months to celebrate

eighty years. Resolute she turned
her slumped face towards the wall

willed her final stroke.
As she could not speak

I voiced her wishes
refused antibiotics

I did not tell her son and older daughter
of the horror when

a fire alarm rang
and suddenly her eyes opened wide.

Paralysed and speechless perhaps
she dreamt she would be burned alive.

I held her hand tightly
said I would never leave her

later understood she always wanted
that I should save myself.

hallux valgus

when the bones of my feet followed yours
I understood we were treading on razors

each morning you forced my feet into
school shoes you'd saved for
each evening you pulled on a plastic rain hood
walked to the bus
trod night shifts along the long corridors
in shoes split by your spreading feet

years after your death mother
I re-trace our scars

ear worms

in the dead of night when I woke
I heard Grace dashing her worries away

steam hissing and spitting as she thumped
the fronts of shirts on a rickety ironing board

wobbling under her pressure
though Percy had tried to mend it with string

I hear her still when I wake in the night
electric and urgent as always

through closed eyes I see
my school frock on top of that pile

Heirlooms

I strain vegetables through
an aluminium colander
more dented now
than when my mother cared for it.

Vegetables are not to blame
though mine are harder than the mush she strained.
She also left me
two glass lemon squeezers.

One splintered on the kitchen floor.
I like to use the survivor though to press out
sharp scent. Pips stick in its teeth.
It is hard to wash up.

All Souls' Night

Last time Mum and Dad visited me
they were both long dead, she
for a decade, he thirty years or more.
Mum wore her warm checked coat,
Dad was in Sunday best, white shirt pressed,
no tie, his hair still red. I poured tea
into their bone china cups
said I'd bake Welshcakes in no time at all
but they weren't stopping. They just called
to kiss me and to give me words of love,
words I'd never heard in all the years before.
Through the thirty nights of November
I longed to welcome them again. The cakes
went mouldy in the tin, the kettle was cold.

river deep mountain high

when my mother came back from the dead
what a hit she was on the chat show circuit

watching her on screen I could see
her navy dress is a touch low cut

sequins glint above a pleat of cleavage
hinting at hidden depths in this old lady

she launches into one of her best anecdotes
how she overcame her vertigo in Japan

climbed up a backstage tower to watch
Ike and Tina Turner in concert

when we went for drinks afterwards
I loved Tina but Ike – years before she
wrote her story I could see he was a shit

the host lays on flattery
now spiked with more curiosity

Grace my darling, you gate crashed a sold-out concert
by two of the biggest stars on the planet
where the hell was security –

he leads the audience in laughter at the very idea
this old lady could have done that

it was hard climbing that tower with my arthritis
but I went with our lovely tour guide –
I won't say her name in case her mother is watching –

and excuse my language but I have to say
she was shagging a security man
so we had access all areas

then Grace sniffs while holding up her book
Saturday's Child Must Work Hard For Its Living

she looks straight to camera and dabs her eyes
with a perfectly pressed white handkerchief

says how very much she wishes
she'd finished writing it before she died

a nano-second of shock glazes
the host's face before he recovers
to keep the chat and the laughter going

Grace I remember you
keeping the chat and the laughter going
gales of hearty laughter was

that cliché you tapped so often
into your tiny Olivetti
as you started to write your story

while I try to sort your pages
to fit each top copy
to three blurry echoes

constantly I hear your voice
and answer back

do I love you, my oh my
mother I love you
like a flower loves the spring
like robin loves to sing

My brother cooks Easter lunch

Golden breadcrumbs shroud
your home-cooked ham
slices share a platter with lamb
pink and just a little bloody.

Cucumber scales sheathe a whole salmon
swimming through swells of parsley.
Tender young prawns
offer themselves up naked and rosy.

We are all hungry and can see
what a feast you had cooked for us
before you said you were nipping out
for cigarettes. An hour passes. Your wife

sends your small daughter to find you
starting at the doors of The Ship. When
at last she steers you home from
The Salutation, you insist we must not eat

until you squeeze a lemon into virgin olive oil
to anoint wilting leaves. You shake in more
salt than you mean. At the table you
push away your plate untouched before

you drain your dark glass, once more
refill then raise it up and slur
a toast to family. One more afternoon
with you, wasted brother, crumbles into dusk.

not telling

details are embarrassing
the tongue-red lid
of a Brylcreem jar
lolls on his dressing table
put it away

at family celebrations
wedding and birthday cakes
I spit out the currants
behave yourself

at family wakes I must
eat then brush away
flakes of rage and shame
say nothing if you can't
say something nice

funeral meats

a terrible hunger seized me
as the curtains closed at the crem
I longed to get to the pub
to eat up the wake for my brother

the eulogies all said
what a good mate he was
all the stories featured
his hilarious drinking

was I the only one
who wanted to cry
over the hungover penguins
who didn't want to laugh

memories fall out
like keys from pockets
of old trousers washed
into holes

so many things mislaid
apparently lost
and yes best
forgotten

nobody mentioned
wages pissed away
nor houses re-possessed
wives left behind
children bewildered

I hand round crisps
crunch pork scratchings
swallow salt and wormwood
keep silence

the day after my brother's funeral

uncapping another bottle of low alcohol wine
I think of the brother you might have been
the one who didn't run away to sea at sixteen
the one who became an artist say,
developing that early talent for drawing
you threw away, discarding it
as carelessly as tossing crumpled paper
into a bin. I pour the blushing wine,
raise my crystal glass to salute
a brother who might still be alive,
who might not have had
so many sorrows to drown,
a brother who didn't groom his little sister
who didn't rape me when I was nine.

Resting

I hope that in his grave my father
has ceased to be disappointed by me.

I hope that my mother, who chose
to have no grave, is no longer

disappointed that student medics
did not take her corpse to parties,

did not give her one last graceful turn
around the dance floor

before they dissected her. I hope
that she is happy that I gave

her ashes to her much-loved son
to scatter on a mountain in Nepal

(where he briefly lived and married his third
and most enduring Yorkshire wife)

a country our mother visited once and said she loved
in spite of the salmonella

which kept her off work for a month.
I hope the ashes of that much-loved son,

my desperate and alcoholic brother,
might gently snow down remorse.

I hope that my big sister and I
before we reach our graves

we may admit how much we love each other
find a way to share memories of sitting up in bed

as she read to me from her Child's Bible
with pictures of a Lord Jesus bleached as white

as those square houses we were taught
Bible people lived in with stairs outside

so they could sleep on the roof on hot nights
we could not imagine in chilly Kent.

I hope to rest under a coverlet of earth
in an ancient churchyard

where pity will rot from my bones and worms
consume my need for absolution.

Notes

A Terrible Resolution: Percy wrote the letters to Grace in 1942, she kept them in a little leather case and left them to me.

In the beginning: The London Blitz was the systematic bombing of the city by the Luftwaffe in 1940 and 1941.

Did anyone else pay to meet Miss Clout? During World War 2 there were seven RAF bases in Kent which was on the front line.

Littlebourne woods: a beauty spot near Canterbury still famous for native English bluebells.

bombing raid and **First meeting imagined:** Percy witnessed the bombing of Canterbury on June 2 1942, called the Baedeker Raid after the German guide books which Hitler was thought to use to choose target cities. It was said he bombed Canterbury in revenge for the RAF bombing of Cologne, part of saturation bombing of German cities organised by RAF commander Sir Arthur Harris, nicknamed Bomber Harris.

Hares: Inkpen is a hamlet in Berkshire where Percy boarded while doing war work, nursing at Hungerford Hospital.

Swifts: the black cylinders contained the oxygen Percy needed in the last months of his life. He was a nurse during the Second World War but returned to coal mining and died from the industrial disease, commonly called miner's lung.

Bath: 'Beau' Nash, a celebrated dandy and leader of fashion, in 1704 became Master of Ceremonies in Bath which was then a rising Spa town.

Hallux valgus: the medical term for bunions, one of those conditions that people laugh at – unless they have suffered from them.

river deep mountain high: is inspired by one of Grace's real-life anecdotes and the Ike & Tina Turner hit, composed by Ellie Greenwich, Jeff Barry and Phil Spector. The last stanza includes lyrics from the song re-arranged.

Resting: Grace has no grave as she had arranged to leave her body to medical research, saying she expected to be taken to parties by student doctors. Later her remains were cremated and returned. The hospital was keen to stress that student doctors treat bodies with great respect nowadays.

Acknowledgements and thanks

Seven of these poems, in earlier versions, have been published in two pamphlets. A Terrible Resolution, Breech, Treat, A Present, Telling and All Souls' Night were published in Aunts Come Armed With Welsh Cakes (Smith/Doorstop 2019). Mother's Arts was published in The Bone Seeker (Mark Time Books UK, 2016) and included in The Everyday Poet, edited by Deborah Alma (Michael O'Mara Books, 2016).

Grateful thanks to poets, mentors, tutors and critical friends who have encouraged and challenged me, in Border Poets and on courses at Arvon, Ty Newydd and those run by the wonderful Ann and Peter Sansom of The Poetry Business. Thanks to staff and fellow students at Manchester Metropolitan University Creative Writing School, especially Anjum Malik who was my dissertation supervisor. This collection is the culmination of three years distance-learning with MMU, some poems formed my final submission for the Master of Fine Arts degree.

Thank you to Anna Dreda who encouraged me to write poetry again after a long silence and to Ross Donlon for enabling me to finally let my poems out through his Mark Time press.

Finally and always, appreciation of my husband Ennis, whose love and encouragement has been unfailing for more than forty years.